This book belongs to

Made in the USA
Columbia, SC
22 December 2024

50500388R00067